Thoughts and Musings

Kristen Christensen

BookLeaf Publishing

India | USA | UK

Presentation by *BookLeaf Publishing*

Web: www.bookleafpub.com

E-mail: info@bookleafpub.com

ISBN: 9789363309203

First edition 2024

To my husband, your unconditional love, belief
in me, encouragement, and random sayings
keep me on my toes. Thank you for showing
me what true love is.

ACKNOWLEDGEMENT

A big thanks to BookLeaf Publishing for this opportunity!

PREFACE

"Life isn't about waiting for the storm to pass. It's about learning to dance in the rain" - Vivian Greene

Nobody Told Me

No one told me

No one told me that when I left you'd take it out on them. No one told me that you would look at these two beautiful girls and only see pawns and objects in your sick twisted games.

No one told me

One day someone did tell me. You were hurting my babies. THEY told me. They had to tell their mother about the horrors they were being subjected to, by someone who is supposed to love and protect them.

I spoke up.

No one listened.

We went to interviews and meetings and these two babies had to tell complete strangers about what's been done to them. To be told their mom is making it up. To be told I. Don't. Believe. You.

No one listened.

Their hardships worsened in degree and they reached out to mom again. So I spoke again.

No one listened.

For 10 years you subjected my perfect, beautiful daughters to hell. Literal hell and got away with it, because nobody would listen to a mother's plea for help. Believing the lies you told about how crazy and vindictive she was.

Why? Why would no one listen?

Finally, one day you slipped up and left visible marks. Then finally, FINALLY someone listened. They don't see you anymore. They want to. It confuses them and devestates them that they miss you but don't at the same time.

But....I listen.

I listen to them when they scream at me and blame me for all of the wrongs in their lives. I listen and I agree that life is so hard and so unfair.

Because no one told me.

No one told me that I'd be awake on a Saturday
night, bawling my eyes out and writing this.
That two years later they'd still be struggling
with not seeing you and hating themselves for it.
That these sweet young women blame
themselves for all the abuse they experienced at
your hands.

No one told me that life would be this damn
hard for my babies. That I'd hate myself so much
over something completely out of my control.
That I'd be completely helpless and scrambling
trying to pick up the broken pieces and help put
them back together again.

So I'm telling myself. This is fucking hard. This
is not my fault. We ALL will get through this
and be the better for it. Because....

Someone's got to tell me.

Today (Adoption Day)

Today

Emotions rolling tears flowing
Big changes in the final stages

Today

Life begins a-new a fresh start
For two precious hearts

Today

Two broken fragile hearts once broken apart
begins to slowly mend thanks to this man's hand

Today

A coward left a mess in his wake, this man here
picked up the pieces knowing what was at stake

Today

Strong and silent never complaining this man
here sets my heart a-flaming

Today

Not one not two but three precious souls he's
saving not once ever wavering

Today

Men without honor left these children without a
proper father. He stepped in without a falter and
proved what it means to be a father.

Today

For once, Today, he will be recognized for all
he's done without expecting a prize.

Today

Always there protecting and steady this man,
Russell, is the definition of a Daddy.

Today

Finally, set free these girls will forever and
always be part of a happy family.

Today

We celebrate these precious souls who've
endured so much and the man who has a heart of
gold who loved them without being told.

Today

Reminder to Self

The number on the scale shouldn't tell you, you FAIL!

The size of your clothes shouldn't scream, you are WORTHLESS!

Every shape and size floats before our eyes.

Do you look at others and scream, "Your weight makes you worthless to me!"?

No? Me either so why do we wither, under our stares in the mirror?

There is more to us than meets the eye, underneath the layers you'll find most people are pretty fly.

If you have a heart of gold and wish to try a new mold, where we appreciate everyone young and old, then start by going bold.

Love EVERY fold! Love the wrinkles, sags, and bits and realize this body is what is keeping you going.

Is it easy? Oh hell no! But we deserve to be
more than our own greatest foe.

Join me in a journey to becoming someone new.
Focus on being healthy and true and maybe soon
we'll all be less blue.

Inner Child

One thing I love about you is your determination
that is true.

You've been through hell and back but you never
fell through the cracks.

You slipped, you stumbled, you were downright
humbled.

But, you knew, you KNEW, deep in your gut
things had to start looking up.

You lived through unbearable pain and trials,
and even though you were tired, you maintained
your smiles.

You never gave up. Being told you weren't
wanted, a problem, and ugly you were used.

You laughed in the face of the abuse. I will rise
above and beyond this you said, shaking your
proverbial fist.

Darling, you'd be so proud of the woman we've
become.

You strive to be happy, optimistic, helpful, and understanding.

Finding knowledge, acceptance, and romance in places enchanting.

Your determination is a huge part of what makes you, you.

Keep on keeping on, proving to yourself and others too, that no one can take that determination from you.

One Night

"Oh my God this feels so right," you think to
yourself then saying, "It's only for one night."

Talking really isn't going well …we can't seem
to get along, not even for a spell.

Hands roving, lips moving, moans ensuing. You
ask yourself, "What the hell am I doing?"

Fall to the bed, clothes removed, heavy
breathing soon resumed.

How can someone who treats me so badly make
me feel so thoroughly consumed?

Again and again you fall into this pit, he treats
you so badly and then he throws a fit.

You undress, he smirks like he knows he's won.
He's good at keeping you under his thumb.

He worships your body so well it feels like a
crime. You get along only when it's sexy time.

Things slowly get worse and you think, "What is this curse?" "I promise I didn't look at him, I promise I didn't take off my ring," you rehearse. "How did I go from someone bad to someone worse?" you ask yourself.

Then think, "Well, the sex made it worth it at first." Now you hate the carnal part of you that loves that thirst.

"I have to get out of here", you realize with a start, "If you don't you're in danger of losing all of your heart."

As you run for your life you think, "This should have just been for one night." The tears fall and as you blink, you decide you'll fight this injustice with all your might.

Smallest Moments

I look at you laying there, your fingers curled
like a fairy's stair.

Peacefully sleeping you softly snore and I
realize how valuable these moments are.

You are mine. I know it's meant to be all of us
together for eternity.

From the way your nose crinkles in disgust to
the crazy hair you sport from a wind gust.

You are each special within my heart and each of
you play a specific part.

Child number one has a huge heart you see

Child number two insists on being organized,
clutter free

Child number three is creative as can be

Child number four spends time in nature,
looking at bees

Child number five is happy when playing wild
and free

A messy face and sticky fingers trace my
happiest memories and bring a smile to my face.

Your births, your milestones, everything about
you exists in my mind, my favorites are the
smallest moments.

Why Me

"Why? Why me?", you cry.

Deep inside a piece of respect for you within me dies.

"Why me" annoys me so, it triggers and angers me as I scoff and try not to blow.

I think to myself, "Does anyone want this trial?......would you want to wish this on someone else? How cruel!!"

"Am I the problem? Why does "why me" bother me? Is this heartless of me?" I wonder as I question myself and my sanity.

So I keep quiet and listen to you wail while trying to not yell.

I know you are hurting and if I could I'd take this pain from you.

I don't think that God purposely punishes us, I think he sends trials to strengthen us.

We all handle things differently so I will listen as you cry "Why me" and I will try to have sympathy.

Kinkle

17

Kindness is something that
I find attractive
No matter who you are
Kindness equals
Love for yourself and for
Everyone else

Eirenicon

Even though life has been rough
I try to look for the good in everyone
Right or wrong it is important to treat
Everyone with grace and sympathy
Not only does it help you to be peaceful
It helps others when you show
Compassion and understanding
Onward and upward we should strive to
Never give up on eachother

Anamorphic

At eight years old I found a lie that
Nearly destroyed me inside
As I tried to decipher right from wrong
My little heart almost gave up
On men. Somehow I found the
Resilience to try and trust men again. I
Prayed for healing and the ability to forgive
Holding onto the thought that not everyone
Is bad. Now I have found someone that I
Can trust and feel safe with, after 25 years.

Enemy

He's not my enemy. I know he's not.

So why do I make him pay for every tear drop?

When I get frustrated and overwhelmed I snap at him.

He graciously takes it and reminds me he loves me.

He is not the one who hit me, screamed at me, and broke me down.

He is the one who encourages me and lifts me up when I am on the ground.

Why do I make him pay like he's the enemy, when clearly he's here to stay?

I try my best to not let the trauma of my past indicate whether he's truly a good man.

On my good days I can identify all the ways he treats me like a queen.

On my down days all I can think is, "Why are all men mean?"

He's not mean, he did nothing bad to me.

You're beautiful, sexy, and a great wife and mother are things he says to me.

It seems too good to be true that a man would be nice to me.

Growing up I heard, you're not wanted, you're a burden, and a curse.

Then when I married young that boy told me I was of no worth.

He screamed at me, hit me, pushed me around, and raped me.

This man has done nothing but tell me how much I am worth.

He has seen me at my worst, he has seen me at my best, and he is my biggest supporter.

It is not fair to him that I struggle to believe the things he says to me.

I know he's not my enemy, he is the greatest
thing that's ever happened to me.

So I will continue to heal and hopefully soon
he'll see, deep down I know he is not my enemy.

Gamophobia

Going to the chapel
And we're going to get
Married.
Oh hell no we aren't,
Please, it's just a piece of paper
Happiness doesn't come from
One getting married.
But then again
I want this man, to be mine
Always and forever, so I'll do it.

Knowledge

24

Keeping up on learning should
Never feel like a chore because
Our brains need the stimulation
While some don't enjoy schooling
Learning can come from other sources
Everyone is capable of learning more
Deciding to learn something new
Gets your brain going and
Excites the body's spirit.

Everyone Loves Kristen

 When a niece or nephew come by and I wrap
them in my arms and happily sigh,

Others get jealous, hurt, and cry, "Why don't you
come to me?"

When the children just smile and then bury their
faces into my neck, hugging me,

Then comes the retort, "Everyone loves
Kristen." It is said with a smile but the tone does
not agree.

Why is it bad if people like me? I try my hardest
to love everybody.

I want people to feel safe when they are around
me.

I've been told by others it comes from a source
of jealousy.

I don't want people to be jealous of me, I want
us all to appreciate each other's individuality.

Being someone that others feel safe and comfortable with is a huge compliment.

Why does it hurt so bad when people say with disdain, "Everyone loves Kristen."

Well I've come to the conclusion it's because it implies that loving Kristen is a bad thing.

Future Self

Future Self

Lose weight, be fit, and have a PH.D,
These are things I'd like for me.

Work on relationships, patience, and
understanding.

Work for 30-35 years for the same company.

But…most of all I hope that

You will love yourself and give yourself grace.

Please don't hate yourself for what you didn't
know. Be proud of yourself, look how much
you've grown!

Word Generater: Leaves, Honor, Waxing

Leaves that are orange, red, and yellow are being shed by trees that are held Hightower the skyline they are full of honor. Showing that fall is Waxing into winter.

Nature

Have you ever walked through the trees and
listened to the birds sing?

How about sitting on the porch as the sun lazily
rises warming the earth with its rays.
Drinking coffee in the slight morning breeze,
reading what ever you please.

Raindrops falling heavily on the rooftop, patter
sounds on the window panes, grab a blanket and
a book, sit by the window, it the perfect nook.

Feeling anxious and alone? Go outside take your
shoes off and walk in the grass soon you'll find
you are calm.

Nature is something that nurtures us all. Many
fail to appreciate and take in all of the earth's
many beauties.

Connection

Disowned and struggling to find a place in this
world

I found a connection in a woman at work who
taught me

That a mother's love doesn't have to come from
love.

She supported me in my hopes and dreams and
talked me through my insecurities.

Here it is twelve years later and problems have
resolved amd relationships have bettered.

That connection is still there though you see. I
sure love this woman, Jackie. You've accepted
me and acted like a second mother to me.

Naps

Sleeping during the day is considered the lazy way.

Napping is frowned upon and people seem to think it is only for the weak.

The way I see it we are all too stressed and burned out so we can't help but sleep.

Buddies aren't meant to be pushed to the max of our physical or mental capabilities.

So I deem, that napping during the day is okay if that is what you need.

Terrifying

32

Things that are terrifying to me are when I have
to explain

Stupid decisions that I made when I was young,
dumb, and reckless.

It terrifies me that those decisions that I made so
many years ago affect THEM today.

My husband and kids shouldn't have to pay for
the mistakes that I made back in my "heyday".

One day soon hopefully everything will be calm
and peaceful like it should be.

Opposites

Often times when we
Play I can't believe, I get to be
Promised to you forever.
Opposites attract is what they
Say. That is the absolute truth
In our case. We are
Together because we appreciate
Each other's differences and can
See that we are just meant to be.

www.ingramcontent.com/pod-product-compliance
Lightning Source LLC
Chambersburg PA
CBHW071235140726
47996CB00007B/2614